150 Years of
Carrubbers Christian Centre

Compiled by
Eric Scott

Latent Publishing

Copyright © 2008 Carrubbers Christian Centre

First Published September 2008 by Latent Publishing

Latent Publishing is an imprint of Latent Publishing Ltd.

Latent Publishing Ltd
P.O. Box 23919
Pathhead, Scotland
EH37 5YG

www.latentpublishing.com

British Library Cataloguing in Publication Data

A catalogue record for this book is available from the
British Library.

ISBN 0-9548821-4-8

Printed and Bound in Great Britain.

CONTENTS

Carrubbers - The Early Years 7

The Work Continues 43

These Last Fifty Years 49

But What of the Future? 69

Carrubbers - The Early Years
Proverbs 10.25 "the righteous is an everlasting foundation."

After Israel's seventy-year captivity, the returnees laid the foundation stones for the new temple, the previous one having been destroyed by Nebuchadnezzar. One of the returnees was an aged prophet by the name of Haggai. After having noted precisely the date on which the foundation was laid, the prophet declared, "Give careful thought to the day when the foundation of the Lord's temple was laid."

Those of us who are now enjoying the benefits and the blessings of Carrubbers Christian Centre would do well to look back and consider the foundations of this great work.

The building which occupies 65 High Street was opened by the American evangelist, Dwight Lyman Moody on 4 March, 1884; however, this was not the beginning of Carrubbers. The work which was originally known as Carrubbers Close Mission was founded 26 years previously on Sunday, 30 May, 1858, and at that time was known as the Experimental Pioneer Home Mission.

A local minister, Rev. James Gall rented premises for the sum of £20 per annum at the lower end of Carrubbers Close. This particular building had once been given the dubious title of "the celebrated cathedral of the prince of darkness". The premises, known as Whitefield Chapel, had been built in 1736 by Alan Ramsey as a theatre. The famous preacher, George

Revd. James Gaul

Whitefield had at one time preached at the theatre and it was thus known as Whitefield Chapel. However, on this particular Sunday morning, Rev. Gall called together three other clergymen in order to form this experimental pioneer work. Rev. Gall had noted that there were many thousands of unreached children living in the vicinity of Carrubbers Close and was firmly of the view that a Sabbath school would be the natural work from which all other evangelistic, civilizing, and benevolent enterprises would most readily branch forth. He firmly believed that children would be the natural means to reach families for Christ and the subsequent story of Carrubbers bore adequate testimony to the accuracy of Rev. Gall's vision.

Carrubbers Close Mission produced a magazine entitled *The Evangelist* and a testimony recorded at that time is worth repeating:

"A youth of about fourteen or sixteen years of age was brought to Jesus at an early stage of the revival meetings. He lived with his father, mother, and sister. Night after night he went home grieved that there should be no family worship at home. One night he could bear it no longer. He spoke to his father about it and entreated him to take down the long-neglected Bible and commence the reading of God's Word. His father put him aside gently at first, but the boy still persisted

Whitfield Chapel

and asked his father to reach down the Bible, 'For', he said, 'if ye'll no' begin, I must do it myself.' This so exasperated the man that he raised his hand and struck his son for what he thought his presumption, and when the boy ran out of the house, peace and quietness were apparently restored. A long silence ensued till the father became somewhat alarmed at the boy's long absence. The night was dark and he was ill at ease till going out to see if he could find him, he heard a voice, as if proceeding from an outhouse and on stealthily approaching, he overheard the boy praying for his poor father who would neither read the Bible nor pray. The father returned in agony to his house. 'Oh wife', he said, 'there's something awfu' gaun to happen. He's oot there praying for his prayerless faither. Oh it's terrible for it's true.' The arrow was directed by a never failing hand. The Spirit had commenced a work of grace in that careless man's heart and he and his wife and daughter were eventually brought to the Saviour through the instrumentality of that little boy. The last time I saw them, they were indeed a happy family rejoicing in the Lord Jesus."

As the children's work advanced, so did other aspects of the work, and God supplied both resources and workers. Under Rev. Gall's direction, the Mission took on several characteristics which were unique in God's work at that particular time as Christians gathered from various denominations to help in the outreach. The workers were not only required to give their labour freely, but also had no monopoly on any one form of the work. They did however, enjoy complete freedom of action to choose, start, or take on work as there was no committee or church government to offer direction. In the circumstances, there was a strong feeling that individuals were responsible to God and not a governing body and therefore such freedom of action was legitimate. There were however, a few basic principles which undergirded all activities. The limited responsibility and freedom of action referred to were designed to encourage inventive evangelism.

A comment made at the time was that "evangelism without sectarianism and inhibition aided its growth and popularity and breadth of labour."

In the early days, the work was assisted by a Mr. Alexander Jenkinson who had a factory and shop at the east end of Princes Street. Mr. Jenkinson founded the firm which later became known as Edinburgh Crystal. He brought to the

Alexander Jenkinson

Mission 150 young women from his factory whom he trained to teach the children in the Sunday School. This teaching session was held every Sunday afternoon at five o'clock. It was recorded at the time that the interest of the young women and their fervent prayers brought great expectancy and blessing to the large gatherings which were held each evening at the Free Church Assembly Hall on the Royal Mile. Mr. Jenkinson's shop in Princes Street became a kind of "house of call" both for his fellow-citizens and for strangers visiting the city who wished to know what meetings were in progress at Carrubbers Close Mission.

The Earl of Kintore who became a great friend of Carrubbers Close Mission, playfully dubbed Mr. Jenkinson the Bishop of Edinburgh.

Alexander Jenkinson's love for souls was beyond measure and whilst Mr. Gall, the founder, was described as the head of the work, the epithet was applied to Mr. Jenkinson as its heart. In 1863, a medical mission and dispensary was set up and it was recorded at that time that 7000 patients were treated annually. Then in 1865 the mission was joined by Professor Sir James Young Simpson who became world-famous as the discoverer of the anaesthetic preparation chloroform, thus the physical needs of the people were ministered to along with their spiritual needs.

Jenkinson's Shop

One of the great features of the Experimental Mission was the dependence on prevailing prayer. On the first anniversary of the mission on May 7, 1859, Rev. Gall declared, "Prayer was the first act and the first breath of the mission and prayer has continued to keep open the windows of heaven from which all this blessing is being poured out." At this time, God was opening the windows of heaven and pouring out blessing in the United States of America. 1857 saw a God-sent revival in the US and by 1858, Northern Ireland was being affected by it.

Professor Sir James Young Simpson

In 1859, this revival blessing spread to Scotland and particularly to Carrubbers Close Mission. In that year, Rev. James Gall visited Glasgow and encouraged by the Christian work he saw there, was urged by the workers and members of Carrubbers to hold a meeting every night. On Sunday, 28

August, 1859, an announcement was made that a meeting would be held every evening until further notice. It was commented fifty years later in 1909 that the day of further notice has not yet arrived. Evangelistic meetings had been carried on without a break of one single evening.

It was at such a meeting on 14 October, 1859 that the first "anxious enquirer" remained behind. This proved to be the first fruits of an abundant harvest, and in the months that followed, it was often with difficulty that the chapel was cleared before eleven o'clock in the evening. So great was the interest that there were many occasions when hundreds had to be turned away from the packed building.

At that time, there was a theatre at the foot of North Bridge. This was subsequently demolished to give way for the building which stands there at present. However, the mission, due to the good offices of the Lord Provost, was given use of the premises for three months prior to demolition. It was recorded at the time that a rich harvest of souls was reaped every evening. When the work commenced, part of the mission premises was used for educational and social operations, however, as the number of enquirers increased, every room was occupied with devotional, prayer or evangelistic meetings. Edinburgh was stirred to its very depths by an anxiety to hear the simple Gospel.

One unique aspect of the work was that there was no popular preacher to attract or arouse the curiosity of the crowds. Instead, the meetings were conducted chiefly by members of the mission. However, in 1859, Carrubbers employed a full-time evangelist, Rev. William Patterson. He travelled widely leading missions and preaching the Gospel. In 1862, it is recorded that he travelled 7000 miles, changed his bed 150 times and addressed at least 500 meetings. In addition, groups from Edinburgh took meetings all over Scotland and many local fellowships were encouraged.

By 1869, the 11th year of Carrubbers' enterprises, there was an average of 50 meetings per week. These meetings were conducted by a little army of evangelistic labourers among whom there was not a single paid agent. Whilst the main aim of the mission was to conduct evangelistic services from the premises in Carrubbers Close, it was one of the outstanding principles of the movement that all the workers should be ready to help every other organization and thus become the servant of all. It is interesting that the revival at Carrubbers affected not only the immediate area but also took on an international flavour. The Evangelist, the Carrubbers periodical, stated that at the time;

"Our organization has spread itself over the whole district like a net and not only has its local influence been great, but among the soldiers on the strands of India, the sailors on the billows, the men and women who have gone to our colonies, there are many who daily thank God for Carrubbers Close Mission."

One important feature of the work during the early years was the use of the Church of Scotland assembly hall. These

Free Church Assembly Hall during Mr. Moody's Visit.

premises were taken over every Sunday evening. During this time not only were the most valuable ministers of the city of Edinburgh used, but distinguished preachers from all over Britain and indeed from North America graced the platform of the assembly hall. The appeal of Carrubbers crossed every denomination and every aspect of social life in the city. Again, *The Evangelist* reports:

"Ministers of nearly every evangelical denomination in the city, evangelists, noblemen, officers of both Army and Navy, laymen of all orders, missionaries from nearly every quarter of the world including African, Indian, Chinese, English, Irish, American and Italian brethren all have been among the speakers this past year."

During these early years, prayer was referred to as the backbone of the work. An article in *The Evangelist* explained the following:

"Every night our work goes on from Sunday till Saturday and has now been going on for more than ten years and still the Lord continues to shower down a blessing. In other places, the revival has been stopped, but in Carrubbers Close, it continues as fresh as ever proving the power and the Scripturalness of the principles upon which it is founded. Let anyone who doubts this visit Whitefield Chapel. He can never come wrong, but especially let him come on a Saturday evening which is especially devoted to prayer and there he will see the secret of our strength in the wrestlings for a blessing which brother after brother engages in one after another until the time is spent. So long as this agonizing spirit of prayer is poured out upon us, it is impossible that the revival can cease among us. It is a most significant circumstance that the most crowded meeting during the whole week is the Saturday meeting where there is nothing but prayer."

A wonderful snapshot has been preserved for us of a Carrubbers prayer meeting. During the mid-1800's, a popular periodical was produced entitled *The Sabbath-School Teachers' Magazine*. A contributor to the magazine visited Carrubbers one November evening and this account has been preserved for us:

"Nightly Meeting in Whitefield Chapel"

Let us describe it. It was past eight o'clock, one dark wet evening in November, that, as invited, we set out for the prayer meeting. We passed down the crowded pavement till, opposite the entrance of a steep close, we were stopped by a gathering of listeners to an earnest street-preacher. There might be about a score of women and girls, with half as many working men and apprentices, standing round the speaker. The men and boys had on their working dress, and were evidently tired with their day's work. They listened respectfully, but without much interest. Hovering round the outside of this knot were

Carrubbers Close 1858

three or four lads, who, as they offered a handbill to any one who might loiter for a few minutes on the street, quietly addressed the words, "Please go to the prayer meeting tonight, in the chapel at the foot of the close."

I got a handbill, and went down the close to the chapel. It is an old building, fitted up originally in the plainest, cheapest manner, and now much worn and sadly in want of light, repair, and paint. The body of the hall was filled with school forms, which might seat 220 or 250 persons, - a narrow gallery would hold sixty more. The gas, however, spread a more cheerful light over it than it could have done through the dingy windows during the day.

On a platform, raised six or eight inches, at the upper end of the chapel, behind a rough deal-table, were ranged five or six chairs. The gentleman who conducted the meeting, and who had originated the mission with which it is connected, occupied the centre seat, while three or four of those who assisted him sat at his side.

The hall was nearly full. Those present were a fair sample of the population of those districts of our large cities which are openly without the profession of Christianity. Near the platform was an old woman, - a well-worn tartan shawl drawn over her shoulders, and fastened round her neck, served the double purpose of warmth and concealment for a gown more

A Caring Community

worn still. Her cap is not very clean, she has no bonnet, but she has brought a pair of spectacles and an old psalm-book, and, having secured a seat near the speaker, she seems as much in earnest as her hard features and dimly lit eyes can express. But we noticed that almost all present had Bibles or Testaments, even yon three ragged 'prentice boys just come from their work have their books. It is not so in our Sabbath schools.

Right before the table, leaning on a stick, even while he sits on the form, is an old decrepit man, thin and shrivelled his eyes rheumy and watery. He was a waiter in one of our most bustling hotels, and seems to have run about till he can now only creep. He must have seen much loose living in these places. A waiter's life is not an enviable one. Yonder sit two strong, toil-stained men, the soil of the anvil still on them. Near them, a mother with a baby at her breast, and a little boy sitting close to her; the key of her house hangs on her finger. In a recess to the left of the platform sit two girls, evidently outcasts: their gaudy wretchedness betrays them, everything about them is arranged as carefully as one would set a snare; but such outcasts were not cast out by Him. The middle seats were filled with a mixture of men and women from the neighbourhood, some children of various ages, and a few well-dressed people. Nearer the entrance are forms filled with groups of work-girls who could not come sooner. You can almost distinguish, by the peculiar gravity and attention, which of the band was probably instrumental in bringing the others, for evidently some of them are not much impressed. Similar knots of work-lads come in sight, and get absorbed in the meeting.

Besides these, sprinkled over the seats, are a number of Christian men and women, who have taken part in the mission work, and are there to gather in the fruit to the Lord's garner.

At half-past eight the prayer meeting begins. There is nothing remarkable in the service except the earnest stillness that pervades it, and the scraps of paper handed up to the chairman requesting the prayers of those present for a husband or a wife, a sister or a brother, a father or a mother, for one or other of these relations, that they may be brought to Christ. It is a feature which shows the healthfulness of the awakening, that those who feel its power seem instinctively to turn to those nearest and dearest to them, and seek their welfare.

There is no regular address. A few verses are read, and a few remarks made, but there is nothing of an exciting nature said. At half-past nine the prayer meeting closes. Any who are anxious for their souls, and wish special instruction, are invited to stay; all other are requested to leave. They stand, and after singing a single verse of the paraphrase beginning, "Oh, may we stand before the Lamb," and the pronouncing of the benediction, slowly the 250 persons present begin to retire. It is five or seven minutes before the chairman's request that the door may be shut, is complied with; and how many anxious inquirers are there left in the room? There must be at least forty or forty-five!

That old tottering waiter has stayed, yon workmen have stayed; some women, eight or ten lads and boys, and some fifteen or twenty girls, of from fifteen to twenty-five years of age. An elder of one of our churches is speaking to yonder two poor girls we noticed before. Are they anxious about their state? He may well speak with them! Gradually he remembers the face of one of them; well does she remember him. She was once his Sabbath-scholar.

There are not above eight or ten persons who will venture to speak to these inquirers; they cannot be dealt with individually, so they are grouped together, - two, three, or four are assigned to each, and a more solemn and more interesting scene begins. The chairman turns to the Bible, and reads the promise, "They shall look on me whom they have pierced, and mourn." He asks, "Are there any here who know that they are sinners, but do not feel their sins? This promise is for them; let them plead it with God. Are there any here who earnestly desire to see and know Christ? This promise is for them; let them take it to God." They all kneel, and solemnly the promise is presented to God and the blessing sought. After three minutes, the voice of the chairman ceases, and he says, "Now, I will not lead your prayers; let each one, on his knees, silently pray for himself." All is hushed to a deeper stillness; and we trust many hearts sought to rise to God then that never sought to do so before. After a few audible sentences more they rise, and each teacher, face to face, turns to those who profess to be anxious to be saved, and seeks to direct them.

No one can know what goes on in theses various groups; but the spectacle of so many saying, by their actions, "What must we do to be saved?" so thoroughly awakened from *indifference, spreads a solemnity on the scene, and makes one feel indeed that, "God is in this place."*

After an hour, the chairman resumes his place and raises a psalm; it is caught up over the room, and after a short prayer the service is announced as over; but it is not easy to limit by minutes the dealings with the anxieties of those who, scattered over the hall, seem as if their work was not yet half completed, and frequently it is much later ere the last inquirer leaves the hall.

With humble gratitude to God for all that we had seen, and earnestly praying for those souls with whom we had conversed, and for a yet richer and richer blessing, we returned home.

Mention has already been made of the world-wide influence of Carrubbers Close Mission. In the fiftieth anniversary booklet, the list of 55 missionaries is recorded who were connected in some way with the Mission. The list includes the name of Mary Slessor of Old Calabar. In the later part of the nineteenth century, Carrubbers became closely connected with the China Inland Mission. This came about through Mr. Alexander Jenkinson's passion for missions. In 1865, Mr. Jenkinson was on the committee of the Perth Convention.

At that time an unknown missionary from China by the name of Hudson Taylor came to the notice of Mr. Jenkinson. It was proposed that the young missionary should address the convention at its annual meeting in September of that year. The convenor complained that having Mr. Taylor would contravene the character of the conference. He pointed out that these meetings were for spiritual edification. However, Mr. Jenkinson and others prevailed and the young missionary was allowed to address the conference.

Hudson Taylor

Hudson Taylor related an incident that occurred when he was travelling by native junk from Shanghai to Ning-po. Among his fellow passengers was a Chinese by the name of Peter who, though acquainted with the Gospel, as yet knew nothing of its saving power. Whilst Mr. Taylor was below deck, he heard a splash and a cry that told him that a man was overboard.

A nearby boatman unconcernedly said, "Yes, it was over there he went down." Some nearby fishermen were requested to immediately drag their nets through the water in order to rescue the drowning man; however, they were completely unconcerned and callously bargained for money before they would agree to use their nets. When Peter was finally recovered, he was, of course, dead.

On Mr. Taylor relating this incident, a burning sense of indignation swept over the great audience. They wondered how anyone on earth could be found so utterly callous and selfish. The congregation however did not expect the challenge which the young missionary put to them. He said, "Is the body then, of so much more value than the soul? We condemn those heathen fishermen. We say they were guilty of the man's death because they could easily have saved him and did not do it. But what of the millions whom we leave to perish, and that eternally?" Many years later, Hudson Taylor, referring to that meeting, spoke of it as the birth of the China Inland Mission. It is not surprising therefore, that Carrubbers became the epicentre of a world-wide missions outreach.

The philosophy of the mission at that time was that anyone who was brought to the Lord should immediately be urged to begin to labour as the Lord enabled them in bringing others to the Saviour. One important aspect of bringing others to Christ was the use of Gospel tracts. It was reported in 1870 that more than 14,000 tracts were distributed on the streets of Edinburgh. *The Evangelist* records many fascinating testimonies of people who were brought to Christ by this means.

Time does not permit to elaborate on any of these stories, save to mention the case of a servant girl who gave a tract to a young man who mocked her and scoffingly said that he would use the tract to light his pipe. Sometime later, the young man was giving his coat away to an impoverished old man, and he decided that before giving it away, he would look through the pockets. Upon doing so, he came upon the Gospel tract. The cover of the tract asked a simple question, "Are you saved?" This strangely convicted the young man. He knelt down in his home and repeated Psalm 23, "The Lord is my Shepherd" and so on, but he had no peace. Then he remembered something the street preacher had said, that one should simply ask the Lord in faith for salvation.

This the young man did and he experienced an unspeakable joy and discovered the preciousness of the Saviour.

Changed lives, of course produced dramatic social changes. The public records for the period 1859-1865 indicate that there was a decrease in the number of people taken in for drunkenness by a massive 50%.

The events which took place at Carrubbers during this period could not, of course, be kept a secret, and the reputation of God's work at Carrubbers spread. In 1872, an American evangelist, Dwight L. Moody, with his co-labourer Ira Sankey visited Edinburgh. Mr. Moody heard of the work at Carrubbers Close Mission and had also been informed that they held an open-air meeting on the Royal Mile every evening.

The evangelist decided that he would put the workers to the test and visited the High Street when it was a particularly wet evening. Even though the weather was so inclement, there was a large number of Carrubbers workers holding forth to the people who were prepared to listen in the rain. Mr. Moody was so impressed with the work of Carrubbers Close Mission that he became closely involved with it.

The year 1872 proved to be a transition period as the Whitefield Chapel which was described as the cradle of Carrubbers, was demolished in order to make way for what is

Dwight Lyman Moody (1882)

Carrubbers Close Mission Directory (1867)

CARRUBBER'S CLOSE MISSION DIRECTORY FOR 1867.

OFFICE-BEARERS.

HONORARY SECRETARY.—Mr William Robertson, 9 Kirk Street.
HONORARY TREASURERS.—A. Melrose & Co., 93 George Street.
GENERAL SUPERINTENDENT.—Rev. James Gall, Moray Manse.
ASSISTANT SUPERINTENDENT.—Mr Alex. Jenkinson, 8 Dundas Street.
With above two hundred other gratuitous agents.

MISSION PREMISES.

WHITFIELD CHAPEL, foot of Carrubber's Close, High Street.
PREMISES under the Chapel—Hall and Class-rooms.
MISSION DRAWING-ROOM and Side Rooms, 19 Carrubber's Close.
MORAY MISSION-HOUSE, South Back of Canongate.
FREE MASONS' HALL, St John Street.
MISSION HALL, Tolbooth Wynd, Leith (and many others).

MISSION DISPENSARY.

SUPERINTENDENT.—Sir James Y. Simpson, Bart., Queen Street.
MEDICAL OFFICER.—Dr John Millar, Albany Street, *with Assistants.*

Attendance given daily in Whitfield Chapel. Upwards of 3000 patients prescribed for yearly. Medicines supplied free. A Committee of Ladies provide attendance from their own number to converse with the patients in waiting.

ENTERPRISES CONNECTED WITH THE MISSION.

SABBATH SCHOOLS.

Morning School, W. Chapel, 9½ o'clock.
Morning School, Moray M. H., 9½.
Children's Service, W. Chapel, 2½.
Afternoon School, M. Hall, Leith, 2½.
Afternoon School, Baker's Place, 4½.
Evening School, W. Chapel & U. Ch. 6.
Evening School, Free Masons' Hall, 6.
Evening School, Painters' Hall, Can. 6.
Evening School, Moray Mission-H., 6.
Evening School, Cowgate Port, 6.

BIBLE CLASSES, &c.

Prof. Smeaton's Bible Class, *Sab.* 9½.
Young Men, Moray Mission-H. *Sab.* 4½.
Young Women, under Chapel, *Sab.* 9½.
Young Women, Drawing-Ro. *Sab.* 5.
Female Servants', W. Chapel, *Frid.* 7.
Italian Bible Reading, 7 Lothian Road.
Bible Reading, W. Chapel, *Wed.* 8½.

PRAYER & PREPARATION MEETINGS.

Sabbath Morning, Whitfield Chapel, 9.
Teachers', under Chapel, *Sab.* 1.
Teachers', under Chapel, *Sab.* 7½.
Teachers', Free Masons' Hall, *Sab.* 7½.
Teachers', under Chapel, *Mon.* 8½.
Teachers', Drawing-Room, *Tues.* 8½.
Teachers', under Chapel, *Thur.* 8½.
Teachers', under Chapel, *Fri.* 8½.
Teachers', Moray Mission-H., *Sat.* 8.
Masons' meeting, M. Dr.-Ro., *Thur.* 7.
Masons' meeting, M. Dr.-Ro., *Sat.* 7.
Young Women, under Ch., *Mon.* 8½.
Young Women, under Chapel, *Fri.* 8.
General Prayer Meet., W. Ch., *Sat.* 8½.

EVANGELISTIC MEETINGS, &c.

Street Preaching, various localities.
Whitfield Chapel, *every night,* 8½.

New Assembly Hall, *Sab.* 6½.
Moray Church, *Sab.* 6½..
Tolbooth Wynd, Leith, *Sab.* 6½.
Duddingston, *Sab.* 6½.
Stenhouse Mills, *Sab.* 6. *Tues.* 6.
Female Meeting, Dr.-Ro., *Sab.* 6½.

Provincial Evangelism. The following places visited by Evangelists:—

Alloa.	Dunfermline.	Leslie.
Anstruther.	Dunipace.	Methil.
Burntisland.	Elphinston.	Methil Hill.
Bonnyrig.	Falkirk.	Marigold.
Burdiehouse.	Gladsmuir.	Musselburgh.
Chirnside.	Golspie.	Paris.
Crail.	Grangemuir.	Pittenween:.
Cockburnspath.	Haddington.	Portobello.
Cumbernauld.	Jock's Lodge.	Preston.
Dalkeith.	Larbert.	St Andrews.
Dundee.	Leven.	Selkirk.
Dunse.	Largo.	Wooler.

LADIES' MEETINGS & DORCAS SOCIETIES.

Mothers' Meeting, Dr.-Ro., *Mon.* 3.
Dorcas Society, under Chapel, *Mon.* 8½.
Dorcas Society, Mis. Dr.-Ro., *Thur.* 7.

SECULAR CLASSES.

Reading,Wr., Arith., &c., U. Ch., *Sat* 5.
Drawing, Exc. Asso., M. M. H., *Mon.* 8½.
French,Y. Men's Inst., M. D. R.,*Mon.* 8½.
French, Exc. Asso., M. M. H., *Tue.* 8½.
Book-keeping, Y. Men's Inst., *Tue.* 8½.
Grammar, under Chapel, *Tue.* 8½.
Vocal Music, under Chapel, *Wed.* 8½.
Vocal Music, Y. Men's Inst., *Wed.* 8½.
Arithmetic, Exc. As., M. M. H.,*Wed.* 8½.
Writing, Ex. As., Chalmers' Cl., *Wed.* 8½.
Drawing, Y. M. Ins., M. D. R., *Thur.* 8½.
Grammar, Exc. Asso., M. M. H., *Fri.* 8½.
Essay-writing, Draw.-Room, *Fri.* 8½.
Social Meeting,Y. M. Ins., D. R.,*Sat.* 7½.

Besides numerous other Meetings and Enterprises of various kinds.

now Jeffery Street. Thus, between 1872 and 1884, Carrubbers had no property of its own for conducting meetings, except for two small flats further up the close from Whitefield Chapel. This was a period of accommodation crisis. Despite this lack of accommodation, the work continued. The first visit of Moody and Sankey in 1873 caused *The Evangelist* newspaper to comment;

"another great wave of grace has just passed over our city and is now washing the spiritual shower of all the country around. A wave so deep and broad that we may say that none such has visited us since the days of Whitefield and Wesley."

Moody and Sankey fitted in well to the Carrubbers scene as the methods adopted by the great evangelist had already been practiced with great success by the workers of Carrubbers since the revival of 1860-63. However, Carrubbers had not been without its critics. Many sincere churchmen viewed the doctrine of instant salvation on believing with some incredulity. However, Mr. Moody, who was a strong and mighty advocate for such a doctrine, emphasised this point in one of his addresses by declaring, "Before the minute hand of the clock shall point to the half hour, any poor sinner in this church may find complete salvation in Christ and the pardon for all sins." During the months of Mr. Moody's visit to Scotland, tens of thousands of ordinary people discovered the truth of these words.

One testimony is worth recording. It will be recalled that prior to Mr. Gall renting the property of Whitefield Chapel, it had

Ira D Sankey

been occupied by an infidel club. The chairman of this club was a Donald McAllan. For many years, McAllan had given great trouble to the workers of Carrubbers Close Mission. However, when Mr. Moody visited Edinburgh, he went to a meeting in the Free Assembly Hall in order to have an argument with the evangelist. Instead of arguing with him, Mr. Moody dealt with him as with a man needing salvation, asking if he had ever heard or known of any man who wished to be saved by Jesus and had come to Him and been refused.

Reluctantly the infidel admitted that he had never known such a case. "No," said Mr. Moody, "the scripture cannot be broken. Do you know we are praying for you and you will yet be converted?" Sometime later in the town of Wick, Mr. Moody met this man again and saw that the Spirit of God was dealing

Moody Preaches in London.

with him. On his return to Edinburgh, McAllan was attending a meeting which was being addressed by James Balfour, a well-known lay preacher in the city, when he suddenly became converted.

The news of Donald McAllan's conversion spread like wildfire. Back in the States, American newspapers heard of this story and denied its truth, but at a meeting subsequently held in the Free Assembly Hall, Mr. Moody told the story of McAllan's conversion and added, "I understand that this former infidel is present in this meeting. If so, will he kindly rise and bear witness to the fact of his conversion?" Mr. McAllan rose near the spot where Mr. Moody had first dealt with him and confessed that he had been the infidel who had formerly opposed the Gospel so bitterly and now declared what great things the Lord had done.

Whilst Mr. Moody was impressed with what he saw of the

work of Carrubbers Close Mission, he stated "you can't run this mission on air". He recognized that the work needed adequate premises. The president of the Mission at that time was a surgeon by the name of Sir Alexander Simpson. He was the nephew of Dr. James Young Simpson. The president along with Mr. Moody commandeered a horse and cart and Mr. Moody and the president standing on the back of the cart with an open sheet were driven around the streets of Edinburgh. As the horse and cart passed the many tenement buildings of Edinburgh, people threw money into the sheet from their windows, and by this unusual method, the sum of £10,000 was collected. At that time, this was a very substantial sum of

Sir Alexander Simpson

money and actually financed the building of the premises at 65 High Street which are still in use to this day.

On Tuesday, 24 April, 1883, the foundation stone for the present building was laid by Mr. Moody. The event received wide coverage in local newspapers. It was observed that the High Street was packed with spectators, and people watched the event from every vantage point possible. Two massive blocks of stone had been prepared, the upper one weighing 2 ¾ tons. A local clergyman, a Rev. Mr. Grant, read a portion of Scripture, then the famous preacher and hymnwriter, Dr. Horatious Bonar offered prayer. At that point, the huge company of people assembled sang "Rock of Ages" and Mr. Moody, with the assistance of workmen, set about the laying of the stone.

Mr. Moody Preaches at the laying of the foundation Stone.

The newspapers recorded that he first deftly spread a large thickness of lime on the lower stone block and then placed within the masonry a jar containing a Bible, a history of the Mission, coins of the realm, and the Edinburgh newspapers.

Following this, the upper block was lowered into position. Having declared the stone well and truly laid, Mr. Moody engaged in prayer, craving blessing on the undertaking. Amazingly, the building was completed in just under a year and on 4 March, 1884, Mr. Moody returned to open the new building in person.

With the new commodious premises, the work of the Mission rapidly increased, both within itself and throughout the city and country. Within a few months, its organization consisted of twenty sections of workers with 58 meetings weekly. In a newspaper report in 1886, that is, two years after the opening

Carrubbers Opening 1884

of the new premises, it was noted that the number of workers, all unpaid, had reached 300.

The newspaper went on to report that the attendances at the meetings were four or five times as many as at the old premises. Also it was calculated that evangelistic addresses undertaken by the Mission in various parts of the city reached no less than four to five thousand persons weekly. At the Gospel temperance meeting on Saturday nights, the average attendance varied from 1,200 to 1,500 and the Sabbath schools were attended by some 500 – 600 children.

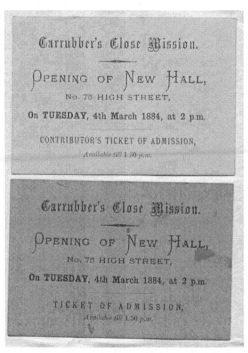

Original invitation tickets from the time of the opening in 1884.

However, this proved to be only the beginning of increased blessing. Carrubbers Close Mission reported in 1887 that the Mission had 500 Christian workers all giving their services gratuitously. The report went on to indicate that during the previous year, more than 920 open-air meetings had been convened, more than 660 indoor meetings , more than 780 prayer meetings, more than 430 Sunday school and Bible study meetings, more than 200 kitchen meetings, more than 290 miscellaneous meetings; in all, above 3,300 meetings. The report concluded by stating that between 8,000 and 10,000 people have the Gospel preached to them every week.

When Mr. Moody travelled back to America, Carrubbers Close Mission was still very much on his heart, and from time to time he sent well-known evangelists and Bible teachers to Edinburgh to assist in the work of the Mission. One of these was a Major Daniel W. Whittle. At the outbreak of the American Civil War in 1861, he enlisted in the 72nd Illinois Infantry and saw much active service. At a severe engagement at Vicksburg, he lost his right arm and was taken prisoner by the enemy. While he was recovering from his wound and having a desire for something to read, he felt in his haversack and found a little Testament his mother had placed there on the morning of his departure for war. The young major read through the book several times, and to his amazement, discovered that he could understand it in a way that he never thought possible. Paul's letter to the Romans gripped his heart and the Holy Spirit brought plainly before his mind that God gave Jesus His Son to be our substitute; and that whosoever would confess their sins and accept Him would be saved.

Whilst the young major was contemplating these things, he was awakened one midnight by an orderly who said, "There is a boy in the other end of the ward who is dying. He has been begging me for the past hour to pray for him, but I'm a wicked man and cannot." The young major said, "But I can't pray. I've never prayed in my life. I'm just as wicked as you are." The orderly retorted, "Why, I thought that from seeing you read the Testament that you're a praying man. I can't go back to the young man alone. Won't you get up and come and see him at any rate?"

Moved by his appeal, young Whittle rose from his cot and went with the orderly to the far corner of the room. A fair-haired boy of seventeen or eighteen lay there dying. There was a look of intense agony upon the young boy's face as he cried, "O pray for me, pray for me, I'm dying. And I'm not fit to die. O, ask God to forgive me. Ask Christ to save me." To use Major Whittle's own words, "I dropped on my knees and held the boy's hand in mine as in a few broken words I confessed my sins and asked God for Christ's sake to forgive me. I believe right there that He did forgive me and that I was his child. I then prayed earnestly for the boy. He became quiet and pressed my hand as I pleaded God's promises. When I rose from my knees, he was dead. A look of peace was on his face and I can but believe that God used him to bring me to the Saviour, used me to get his attention fixed upon Christ and to lead him to trust in His precious blood. I know I will meet him in heaven."

As a result of this incident, Major Whittle wrote the hymn

which subsequently became famous;

"I know not why God's wondrous grace to me hath been made known,
Nor why unworthy Christ in love redeemed me for His own.
But I know whom I have believed and am persuaded that He is able
To keep that which I've committed unto Him against that day."

By the time of Major Whittle's visit to Edinburgh, he was a household name in America and had become well-known in Britain as a hymnwriter and a Gospel preacher. The major became a great favourite at Carrubbers Close Mission and was instrumental in giving a tremendous boost to the Temperance Movement generally, but especially to the Saturday Night Temperance Meeting which was held each Saturday evening in the Mission.

One of the great blessings which came to Carrubbers during this period was that of music in the form of Gospel hymns. These were made popular through the ministry of Ira D. Sankey who always accompanied Mr. Moody on his evangelistic tours. Not only did Mr. Sankey compose many hymns, but he also compiled the best hymns of the time in a hymnbook which became world famous. Many of Major Whittle's hymns were included in this compilation.

Major Daniel W Whittle

One hymn which became a particular favourite was composed under very unusual circumstances. In 1874, Moody and Sankey were travelling by train from Glasgow to Edinburgh. Later in the day they were holding a meeting in the Free Assembly Hall in Edinburgh.

Whilst on the train, Mr. Sankey came across a poem written by Mrs. Elizabeth Clephane.

Mr. Sankey read the words to his friend Mr. Moody which were as follows:

"There were ninety and nine that safely lay
in the shelter of the fold,
but one was out on the hills away,
far off the gates of gold,
away on the mountains wild and bare,
away from the tender Shepherd's care."

Mr. Moody did not appear to indicate much interest in the poem and the two men proceeded to the meeting. Mr. Moody preached on the Good Shepherd and at the conclusion of his sermon asked Mr. Sankey to sing something appropriate. Ira Sankey remembered the poem which he had placed in his vest pocket. Taking out the words, he set them before him on his little organ and improvised the tune on the spur of the moment. The song made a great impression on the congregation and immediately became a great favourite. The organ that Mr. Sankey used on that occasion was kept in Carrubbers until the 1950's when it was bought by the Billy Graham Organization. The organ is now in the Billy Graham Museum in America.

The 50th anniversary of the Mission proved to be a landmark event. It was declared that God's blessing on the work was continuing unabated. A report on the work indicated that a public meeting was held in the premises at 65 High Street on every evening of the year, and also the Gospel preached in the open air on every evening to the crowds on the High Street.

Furthermore, in order to accommodate the crowds, the Free Assembly Hall had been commandeered for Sunday evening services. Looking back over the first fifty years of the Mission, it was reported that it could not be estimated the number of people who were reached and saved through the Gospel message. It was underlined, however, that the founders of the Mission had provided the present generation with a great heritage. Also, it was recorded that special thanks were given to God for His servant, Mr. Moody, who had the foresight and drive to make provision for the premises at 65 High Street.

The next fifty years – 1908-1958
The Work Continues

The 50th year celebration was marked at a special jubilee service in Carrubbers on 30 May, 1908. The renowned surgeon Professor Sir Alexander R. Simpson, nephew of the late Dr. James Y. Simpson, presided and addressed the evening service. On Sunday afternoon, 31 May, 1908, there was a large demonstration held on Carlton Hill preceded by a march from the West End of Princes Street. The final jubilee service was held in the Assembly Hall and again Sir Alexander R. Simpson presided. Sadly, this great and godly man died in 1916. He preached for the last time at Carrubbers on 2 April, 1916 and his text, appropriately, was from 2 Corinthians 5:10;"For we must all appear before the judgement seat of Christ."

During the dark years of the First World War many young men who had been workers at Carrubbers fell in battle. Between the two wars, however, the work of evangelism and Bible teaching continued. During this period, there was great revival blessing in the north of Scotland under the ministry of evangelist Jock Troop. During the period from the 1920's to the 1950's, Mr. Troop held several missions in Carrubbers and on each occasion there was adequate evidence of God's blessing upon them.

Many stories could be related as to remarkable conversions, but one stands out in particular. On this particular occasion, Jock Troop was living in the small flat in the top of the building known as the prophet's chamber. One evening he found it

Jock Troop

impossible to sleep, so he got up, dressed and walked down the Royal Mile to the Queen's Park. He stopped in front of the rocky outcrop known as Salisbury Crags and at the top of his voice, proclaimed the well-known text, John 3:16;

"For God so loved the world, that He gave His only begotten Son that whosoever believeth in Him should not perish but have everlasting life."

Mr. Troop then walked back to the mission premises and reported that following the incident he had a good night's sleep. The following evening after the Gospel rally, one of the enquirers, a lady in her 30's, asked to speak to the evangelist. She related that the previous night it had been her intention to commit suicide and she had stood at the top of Salisbury Crags with the intention of leaping to her death. When she was about to do this, she heard the voice of an angel proclaiming a message of God's love. Mr. Troop, with a wry smile, informed the lady that it was no angel that gave the message. He explained to this distraught woman how he had been constrained to visit the park that evening and proclaim the Gospel text. That woman trusted Christ and discovered the peace that passeth understanding.

Another notable evangelist during that period was Mr. Seth Sykes of the Tent Hall, Glasgow. He convened many missions in Carrubbers and often at the close of the service, in giving the invitation, would exclaim "Will ye no tak' Jesus hame with you?" Many responded to this message and there were many notable conversions. At the outbreak of the war in 1939, Carrubbers was confronted with many new problems. Mr. Robert Miller who was superintendent of the Mission at that time, died in 1940. His place was subsequently filled in 1941 by the Rev. E. Buckhurst Pinch. His ministry was noted for his stirring messages on the Lord's second coming. He convened prophecy meetings on Sunday afternoons when the main auditorium was packed to capacity.

Rev. Dr. David Earl Laurie was appointed superintendent in 1943. Dr. Laurie held special meetings for servicemen when the Oak Hall would be packed with members of the Armed Forces. Many young men came to a saving knowledge of the Lord during this period. Dr. Laurie was born in the Oatlands district of Glasgow and in his early years had no thought of God, but was intent on pursuing the pleasures of this life. However, as a young man he was arrested by the Gospel message and became a fearless preacher of the Gospel. Dr. Laurie was brought up in a Glasgow tenement, and after his conversion he would stand in the back court of the tenement premises where he lived and preached the Gospel.

Dr. Laurie was known as a tender-hearted, sympathetic type of person and sadly, there were occasions when some visitors to Carrubbers would endeavour to take advantage of his

Seth Sykes

sympathy. In those days there was a large tenement block opposite Carrubbers Close Mission and one of the occupants arrived at the door of the Mission at the close of a Sunday evening service. She declared to David Laurie that her husband "was deid" and that she needed financial help. Dr. Laurie promised that he would visit her in her home after he dismissed the congregation. When the superintendent entered the home of this lady, he noticed that her dead husband was lying on the bed covered with a sheet. His feet were protruding from under the sheet and as he passed the corpse, he decided to stroke the sole of the man's feet whereupon the dead man suddenly rose up. Dr. Laurie would often relate this incident as the time when he was able to raise the dead.

In 1945, during the time of Dr. Laurie's ministry, he invited a "Youth for Christ" team from the USA. The team included some of America's outstanding preachers, namely Dr. Torrey Johnson, Dr. Straton Shufelt, and a young evangelist by the name of Billy Graham. It is believed that the very first preaching engagement Billy Graham had in Britain was in Carrubbers Close Mission.

On 27 December, 1955, the work at Carrubbers was disrupted as a result of a serious fire in a building adjoining Carrubbers. It was only due to the providence of God that the building was not completely destroyed. The building was reopened on 28 April, 1956 with much thanksgiving to God for His provision.

These Last Fifty Years

In 1958, Carrubbers celebrated 100 years of ministry. Special meetings were arranged from 21 May to 1 June and many outstanding speakers took part during that period. On 1 June, 1958, the service was broadcast by the BBC, thus the centenary year along with this provided great impetus to the work at Carrubbers. The new era witnessed renewed dedication to Christ on the part of the workers and people in general. Carrubbers became, in a new way for many, a centre of wonderful Christian fellowship and witness where faith was quickened.

Added to the centenary gatherings were the memorable meetings connected with the all-Scotland crusade which brought

Dr Billy Graham at McEwan Hall with Rev D Read

new spiritual life to many churches. The Kelvin Hall in Glasgow was the main venue for the crusade where many thousands flocked to hear the preaching of evangelist Billy Graham. Again this provided a boost to the work at Carrubbers for it was here that Dr. Graham had preached at his first visit to the UK. Following the centenary celebrations, plans were made for further outreach in conjunction with the Tent Hall Mission in Glasgow, which, similar to Carrubbers, had been brought into being by the ministry of D.L. Moody. In April 1960, there was a joint evangelistic campaign and the Rev. John Moore, who was superintendent of the Tent Hall at that time, led the meetings at Carrubbers. At this time, Rev. Stanley Collins was

Dr Billy Graham at Tynecastle - With wife and Rev Dr G Gunn

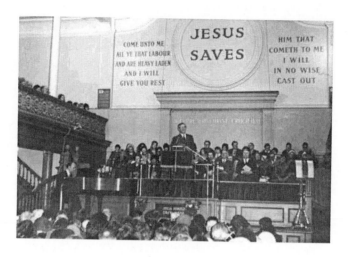

John Moore

superintendent of the work at Carrubbers and the work prospered under his ministry. It is interesting that in 1971, John Moore became superintendent of Carrubbers Close Mission.

In May 1961, superintendency of the work was taken over by Rev. J. Burnett Binnington. Rev. Binnington, of Methodist background, was well-known in evangelical circles. As a young man, Rev. Binnington had accompanied the famous evangelist Gypsy Smith on his extensive evangelical tours as the evangelist's pianist.

It is most incredible, how in God's Providence, events can go full circle. In 1874, Mr. Moody, along with the singer, Ira D. Sankey, were holding meetings in London. As they were taking a drive through Epping Forest, they came upon a gypsy camp. While they stopped to speak to two brothers who had been converted and were doing missionary work amongst the gypsies, a few gypsy lads approached the carriage in which Mr. Moody and Mr. Sankey were sitting. Mr. Sankey put his hand on the head of one of the boys and said, "May the Lord make a preacher of you, my boy." Fifteen years later, Gypsy Smith visited America as an evangelist and singer. Subsequently, Gypsy Smith met up with Ira Sankey. The young evangelist said, "Mr. Sankey, do you remember meeting me?" Of course, Mr. Sankey could not recollect having met the young man in the past. It was then that Gypsy Smith reminded him of the incident in Epping Forest and took the opportunity of thanking Mr. Sankey for that prayer which had been wonderfully fulfilled.

In 1971, Rev. John Moore, previously of the Tent Hall, and now Dr. John Moore, took over superintendency of the work. Dr. Moore at that time was well known in Scotland as an evangelist and Bible teacher and his presence gave a much needed boost to the work. During Dr. Moore's term of office, a free breakfast outreach was commenced for the homeless, which is still operating to this present time. Sadly in 1974, Dr. Moore felt called to another charge, and the work was without a full-time superintendent until 1983. This period probably was the most difficult in the history of Carrubbers. However, the ministry of outreach and Bible teaching continued.

In 1981, evangelist Dick Saunders was invited to convene a city-wide crusade in the area known as the Meadows. The evangelist had available a huge cathedral tent, as it was called, accommodating about three thousand people. The meetings were very well attended and got favourable comments from

Tent used for Dick Saunders Event

the local press. God blessed the ministry and over the period of the crusade, some 500 people responded; more than half of them committing their lives to the Lord for the first time. It is known that several people from this 1981 crusade are now serving the Lord in full-time service.

Two further crusades were convened, one in 1983 and another in 1986. During the period of the vacancy, which was the longest in the history of Carrubbers, the Mission had received help from many areas. The weekly Saturday rallies were the main feature of the work at that time, and during the course of the vacancy, the mission was able to engage many of Britain and America's finest preachers. These included such men as Dr. Dwight Pentecost, Rev. Stephen Olford, Rev. Allan Redpath, Dr. Francis W. Dickson, Rev. D.M. Russell-Jones, Rev. Ronald Park, Rev. George B. Duncan, Major Ian Thomas and a host of others.

During the difficult years of the vacancy, the workers at Carrubbers were much encouraged by a text which came to be known as 'Mr. Moody's Text', which was discovered in the most unusual way. In the late 70's it was decided to redecorate the Main Hall and during the course of the workmen removing the grime from some of the walls they came across a text chiselled into the stonework immediately above the side entrance below the gallery. The text was taken from the prophecy of Isaiah chapter 27: verse 3;

"I the Lord do keep it.
I will water it every moment lest any hurt it.
I will keep it night and day."

Mr. Moody's text - Isaiah 27:3

At the time this text was discovered the work was going through a particularly difficult period and there were pressures from several quarters to close down the work completely. During that difficult period it was felt that this was confirmation from God's word that heaven still had a purpose for the mission. Since that time there has been clear evidence that the work has been kept by the Lord, that He has indeed watered it every moment and kept it night and day. We give God the glory for this.

The long vacancy came to an end when the superintendency was taken over by Rev. K. Skelton in May 1983. In January 1986, Rev. Brian Russell-Jones was called to be minister and superintendent. He was able to bring to the work a sense of stability combined with evangelism and a solid Bible-teaching programme. The work again began to flourish under Rev. Russell-Jones' ministry.

Prior to this new era, a lot of prayer and thought had gone into the future of the work. It was decided that the work could not continue as a mission, relying on outside workers from other churches. The evangelical scene had changed dramatically from the early days of the Mission and there were no longer the people available who would be prepared to give time and effort for the work of the Mission. It was decided therefore, that the

Interior of Carrubbers Main Hall
before the refurbishment

ethos of the vision of the early days of Carrubbers would continue, but this would be operated on the basis of Carrubbers functioning as a church organisation with permanent members. Under Rev. Brian Russell-Jones' ministry therefore the work went forward on this basis.

During this period, it was felt that the premises as they stood were totally unsuitable for the future of the work as envisaged. After several meetings, it was agreed that we should go forward with extensive refurbishment and renovations under the title of "Carrubbers into the Nineties". Mr. David Scott, architect, produced design drawings which featured a mezzanine floor dividing the large hall into two, an upper main auditorium and lower rooms which could be opened on weekdays. This matched amazingly the original vision expressed by Mr. Moody when he opened the building in 1884. He said, "First of all, I would have the place opened from ten in the morning till ten at night, all day. Have the rooms kept warm and cheerful, give the people the best cup of coffee to be found in Scotland." With the Carrubbers Café operating in the lower area of what was the main sanctuary, Mr. Moody's vision has surely been fulfilled.

When David Scott drew up the plans, it was estimated that the cost of phase one relating only to the main sanctuary would be of the order of £140,000. In 1987 when the proposals were put to the congregation, this estimate was far beyond the resources of the fifty or so people actively involved in the work at that time. It was believed however, that it was God's will that the work should proceed and it was recognised by the few people involved, that the God they served was a God with infinite resources.

Thus, the needs were brought before God's throne and on Friday, 4 December 1987, there was convened the first in a series of half-nights of prayer. This ran from 7.30pm until 12 midnight. This was followed by a Gift Day which raised £4,000 and a promise of a further £14,000 by an American pastor Mike MacIntosh who had the previous year conducted an evangelistic mission at Carrubbers. Incidentally, this promise was fulfilled five years later when Mike's church sent Carrubbers the sum of £19,600. This generous gift paid for all of the chairs which are at present in the main sanctuary. At that time, the directors felt that they should ask God for an initial sum of

Bob MacIntyre, David Scott & Chris West
(left to right)

Refurbishment work commences

£100,000 before the work could go ahead. It was felt that this would be a tangible and practical evidence of His will. In November 1988, an unexpected and unforeseen legacy of £64,000 was received. This was the sign for which the directors had been looking. Bank interest and other gifts brought the fund up to the required amount of £120,000 by September of 1990. During that year, permits were sought and estimates secured. However, there were events taking place behind the scenes completely unknown to the directors, but known to God.

Sometime, possibly in 1987, an American visitor arrived in Edinburgh's Waverly Station. At that time Carrubbers had a very large poster advertising the Saturday night rallies.

The American visitor, Mr. Bob MacIntyre, was attracted by the advert and decided to see what type of place Carrubbers was. By profession, Mr. MacIntyre was a skilled interior designer and had previously run his own business in the USA. However, having felt that he was called of God to go into full-time ministry, he joined the Greater European Mission which specialized in providing work teams for Christian work in Europe.

When Bob MacIntyre entered the Carrubbers building, he was amazed at the size of the interior and immediately his expert eye recognized that much could be done to improve the premises. He prayed silently that if ever any renovation work was carried out on the premises, that God would involve him in the project. However, he covenanted with God that he would never openly disclose this to anyone so that if a request for help was made, he would know it was from the Lord.

The remainder of the story reads like a romance. In 1988, Rev. Brian Russell-Jones was invited to preach in Belgium where Bob MacIntyre was living at that time. Amazingly, he stayed at the home of Bob MacIntyre. Nothing was said about the Carrubbers project until the point when Rev. Russell-Jones was actually leaving to return to Edinburgh. Just before they parted company, Brian mentioned to Mr. MacIntrye a little about the vision for Carrubbers and also remarked on the fact that Bob had expertise in the area of interior design. In the last moments before parting, Rev. Russell-Jones asked if any help could be provided. It was at this point that Bob MacIntyre related the incident that had taken place that Saturday evening
some time previous and of the prayer he had made to God for

Different stages during refurbishment

the privilege of helping with such work in the future. Very soon the directors arranged a meeting with Bob MacIntyre and not only did Carrubbers receive free expert help, but work teams were provided from America under the direction of Mr. Carey Holmquist.

During the years which followed, many thousands of work hours were given to Carrubbers free of charge, and in addition, the workers provided finance for the work in which they were engaged and also finance for their accommodation. Without the help of Bob MacIntyre, Carey Holmquist, and the friends of the Greater European Mission, the work could not have been undertaken.

During this time, revised estimates from contractors were obtained which indicated that £400,000 would be required for the basic work in the main sanctuary. This was far beyond the means of Carrubbers. At this very time, a friend of Carrubbers, Drumond Sceales approached Mr. Scott Sr. at the close of one of the Saturday night meetings. He indicated that he had just recently retired and that retirement was not agreeing with him. He asked if he could be involved in the renovation work at Carrubbers. Not only was Drumond Sceales a skilled carpenter and cabinetmaker, but prior to his retirement, held a senior position with Edinburgh District Council's Department of Building Control. It was decided that with Drumond Sceales' help, the directors would have the work carried out employing direct labour.

At the same time, a valued director, George Scott had retired from full-time employment and offered his services as a skilled electrician. Both of these men gave the best years of their retirement for the work of Carrubbers completely free of charge. Both of these men are with the Lord, but we should continue to thank God for their valued services as the work could never have been completed without their help. Trevor Gould also provided help with regard to the electrical work and Chris West, another of the Carrubbers' directors, had the sound and telephone systems installed under his supervision. Two young men, Neil Smith and Graham Lumsden, were employed directly as joiners on a regular basis. The quality of their work is still visible to this day.

The new stained-glass window

The work commenced on October 29, 1990 with all of the labour being provided on a voluntary basis. To start destroying what was really a very attractive Victorian auditorium could only be described as traumatic. The very platform on which

Mr. Moody had delivered his first message at the opening of the premises on the text, "Come onto me all ye that labour and are heavy laden, and I will give you rest," had to be completely dismantled. However, it was quickly recognized that God is more interested in living stones than the bricks and mortar of a past generation.

When the hall was originally constructed, there was a rose window on the back wall of the building. It had, however, been boarded up for many decades. This was reopened and a new stained-glass window constructed. The window was produced and directed by Edinburgh artist, Sandy Parker. The window depicts a cross and Bible linking heaven and earth together in rich blue, crimson, green and gold colours.

Eventually the hall was reopened on March 27, 1992. Drumond Sceales mentioned that during the course of the rebuilding, he was deeply conscious that a Divine hand was bringing resources, finances, and much good will together to achieve a result that could be described without exaggeration as a miracle of God's providence.

"The task is great because this structure is not for man, but for the Lord God."

1 Chronicles 29:2

The opening service was a memorable occasion. The new hall was packed to capacity. The Emmaus Choir took part under the leadership of James Monihan who at one time had been a director of Carrubbers, and Rev. Derek Prime of Charlotte

The opening service

Revd. Wayne Sutton (top)
Revd. Brian Russel Jones (bottom)

Chapel gave the message. There was a deep sense of God's presence and guiding hand.

However, much work was still to be completed. There was still considerable work to be done on the lower portion of the building, namely the café, lower hall, and toilets. Also the upper part of the building, the Oak Hall, library, offices and so on, had not yet been tackled. In January 1994, the money in the building fund dropped to the sum of £20 and it was decided that the work should not proceed as it had already been agreed by the directors that the work would not incur any debt. However, at the beginning of February 1994, Tom Sim, a friend and supporter of Carrubbers over many years, was suddenly called into the presence of his Lord. He had made Carrubbers the sole beneficiary of his estate consisting mainly of the house in which he lived. The sale of this house realised £61,000. Following this timely gift, the work was able to proceed to completion.

While all of this was going on, God was working on the life of a young man on the other side of the Atlantic. In the late 80's, a young man by the name of Wayne Sutton was studying at the Capital Bible Seminary. At this time, Wayne was attending the Maclean Bible Church. In 1989, Wayne visited Carrubbers on a summer missions trip. This was followed by a seven-week visit the following year and took the form of a placement from his seminary. Subsequently, Wayne was invited back to Carrubbers as a missionary with support-backing from friends in the USA. Thus, Wayne arrived back in Carrubbers in 1991 with the promise of five years support. Wayne subsequently married Sarah, the daughter of Trevor Gould, director, and after Brian Russell-Jones left to take up a work in Belgium, Wayne was appointed pastor in 1996.

Since the time that Brian Russell-Jones was appointed as pastor and superintendent, God has blessed the work and God's blessing continued apace following the appointment of Wayne Sutton. The main auditorium is regularly filled to capacity on a Sunday morning and there are presently some twenty-six ministries operating within the organisation. Over recent years, there has been a great interest in missions and there are presently some twenty-four young people involved in overseas work. At present, Carrubbers employs Rev. Wayne Sutton as senior pastor and Rev. David Anderson as associate pastor. Eric John Scott is the president and chairman of the directors.

But what of the future?

On the tenth anniversary of Carrubbers Close Mission, a small booklet was produced which, among other things, related the circumstances through which the Mission came into existence. Under the heading, Origin of the Mission, the booklet records the following:

"The Carrubber's Close Mission owes its origin to a movement which took place so far back as 1855, when the Sabbath-school teachers, in a number of places in England, made what they called a "general canvass" of their respective towns, to find out the neglected children, and bring them into the Sabbath-school. Following their example, the friends of the young in Edinburgh formed themselves into a committee for a similar purpose; the town was divided into seventy-six districts, and visited, during the first week of April 1856, by about a thousand Sabbath-school teachers and others, who entered about twelve thousand houses, containing about twenty-three thousand children. When the returns were given in and collated, it was discovered that there were at least eight thousand of these young persons growing up without any religious instruction whatever."

The article goes on to state;

"The delivery of this report to the Sabbath-School Teachers' Union, which originated the movement, threw upon them a very serious responsibility; because, having obtained the information which they sought, the question still remained, what

were they to do in order to remedy so great an evil? – this responsibility being increased by the consideration that these eight thousand young persons represented an entire section of society which had broken loose from all religious ordinances and Christian profession, and which consisted, probably, of not fewer than thirty thousand souls."

We can now look back with gratitude to those godly people who took up the challenge and formed an outreach mission which reached not only thousands of the children referred to, but also to their parents and to many, many others much further afield. If a similar survey was carried out today, what would the results be? There is absolutely no doubt that the figures would be infinitely worse than they were a hundred and fifty years ago.

In the circumstances, a huge challenge faces God's people at the present time. In Romans chapter ten, the apostle Paul reminds us that there is only one hope for this lost world, and that is the Gospel of grace. In verses fourteen and fifteen, the apostle asks four pertinent, rhetorical questions.

First the apostle Paul states, "How can they call on the One they have not believed in?" The answer is: they cannot call. Then he asks, "How can they believe in the One of whom they have not heard?" Again, the answer is: they cannot believe. Thirdly the apostle asks, "How can they hear without someone preaching to them?" The obvious answer is: they cannot hear. Then fourthly, the apostle asks the penetrating question, "How can they preach, unless they are sent?"

It can be seen from this passage that the world's greatest

need is for God's people to hear God's call and go forth and preach this glorious gospel message. Again, the apostle reminds us in verse seventeen, that faith comes from hearing the message, and the message is heard through the Word of Christ. The Lord Jesus said, "As the Father has sent Me, even so, send I you."

Facing a task unfinished,
that drives us to our knees,
a need that, undiminished,
rebukes our slothful ease.
We who rejoice to know Thee,
renew before Thy throne
the solemn pledge we owe Thee,
to go and make Thee known.

We bear the torch that, flaming,
fell from the hands of those
who gave their lives, proclaiming
that Jesus died and rose.
Ours is the same commission,
the same glad message ours,
fired by the same ambition,
to Thee we yield our powers.

O Father who sustained them,
O Spirit who inspired,
Saviour, whose love constrained them
to toil with zeal untired.
From cowardice defend us,
from lethargy awake!
Forth on Thine errands send us,
to labour for Thy sake.

Frank Houghton (1894-1972)
© Overseas Missionary Fellowship

Those who are wise will shine like the brightness of the heavens; and those who lead many to righteousness, like the stars for ever and ever.

Daniel 12:3

Some of the Children whom Mr. Moody led to righteousness.